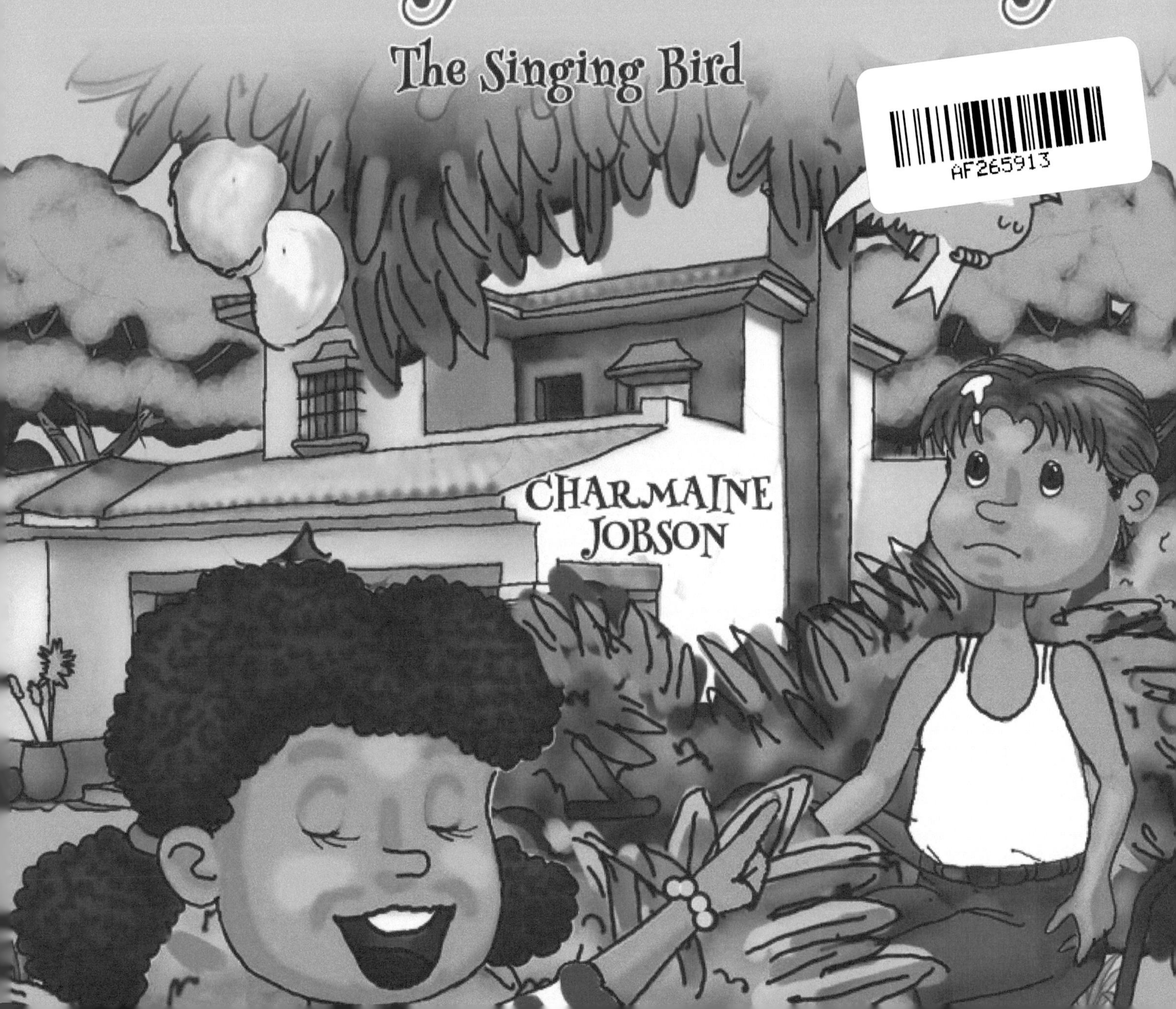

Chatty McNally
The Singing Bird
CHARMAINE JOBSON
AF265913

Chatty McNally
The Singing Bird

Copyright © 2018

Published 2018 by Charmaine Jobson

Illustrations by: J. Gutierrez

Cover designed by: Kent Locke
Book layout by: www.diverseskillscenter.com

U.S. Copyright Reg No. **Case #:** 1-6221105467 (pending)

Printed in the United States of America
ISBN-13: **978-1985652439**
ISBN-10: **1985652439**

**For Paul
With love
C.J.**

Hooray for summer vacation!
Every summer, Peter and Chatty
McNally spend their vacation at
Grandma Lou's house. Grandma lives
in the country on a hill overlooking
the ocean. It is a beautiful farm with
many fruit trees, animals and pretty
flowers.

Her favorite flowers are roses.
She tended them with lots of love
and care. Sometimes she would even
speak to them and call them by
name.

"Grandma, how come you speak to the flowers but they never answer you?" asked Chatty McNally. "Well, they don't speak my dear. I speak, and they listen." Grandma Lou said with a smile.

"I tell them how beautiful they look, how sweet they smell, and I thank them for making my garden a home for many gorgeous butterflies."

Just then, Peter ran over to me. "Come on, hurry up. Let's go play. I just saw a pretty little bird up in the mango tree and it was singing my name." shouted Peter.

"Let's catch it." Peter said as we started climbing up the tree, going from branch to branch.
"He is calling my name; don't you hear him?' asked Peter.

"Shhh! Listen." said Peter in a quiet voice. "He is singing, Peter Come for This. Peter Come for This."

"No! He's not! Birds don't sing. They chirp." said Chatty McNally,
Just then, the bird flew over the branch where Peter was sitting, dropping poop right on top of his head.

Haha.... you look funny! Well, you said he was chirping "Peter come for this." Chatty McNally couldn't stop laughing. Peter was not amused.

When they got home, Chatty McNally
told Grandma about the little yellow
and brown bird pooping on Peter.
Peter was not too happy.

"Grandma Lou, can birds sing?"
asked Chatty McNally, "Peter said
the bird was singing, Peter Come for
this."

Grandma Lou laughed. "That bird is a male Yellowhammer, and it has a lovely voice. The brown ones are female, and the yellow ones are male."
"But Grandma, was he really calling Peter?" asked Chatty McNally.
"Don't believe everything you hear," said Grandma.

"What does that mean?' asked Peter.
"It means not everything you hear is true." "You wanted to believe it was singing your name
Peter but it was really singing a melody to attract the female's attention." said Grandma.

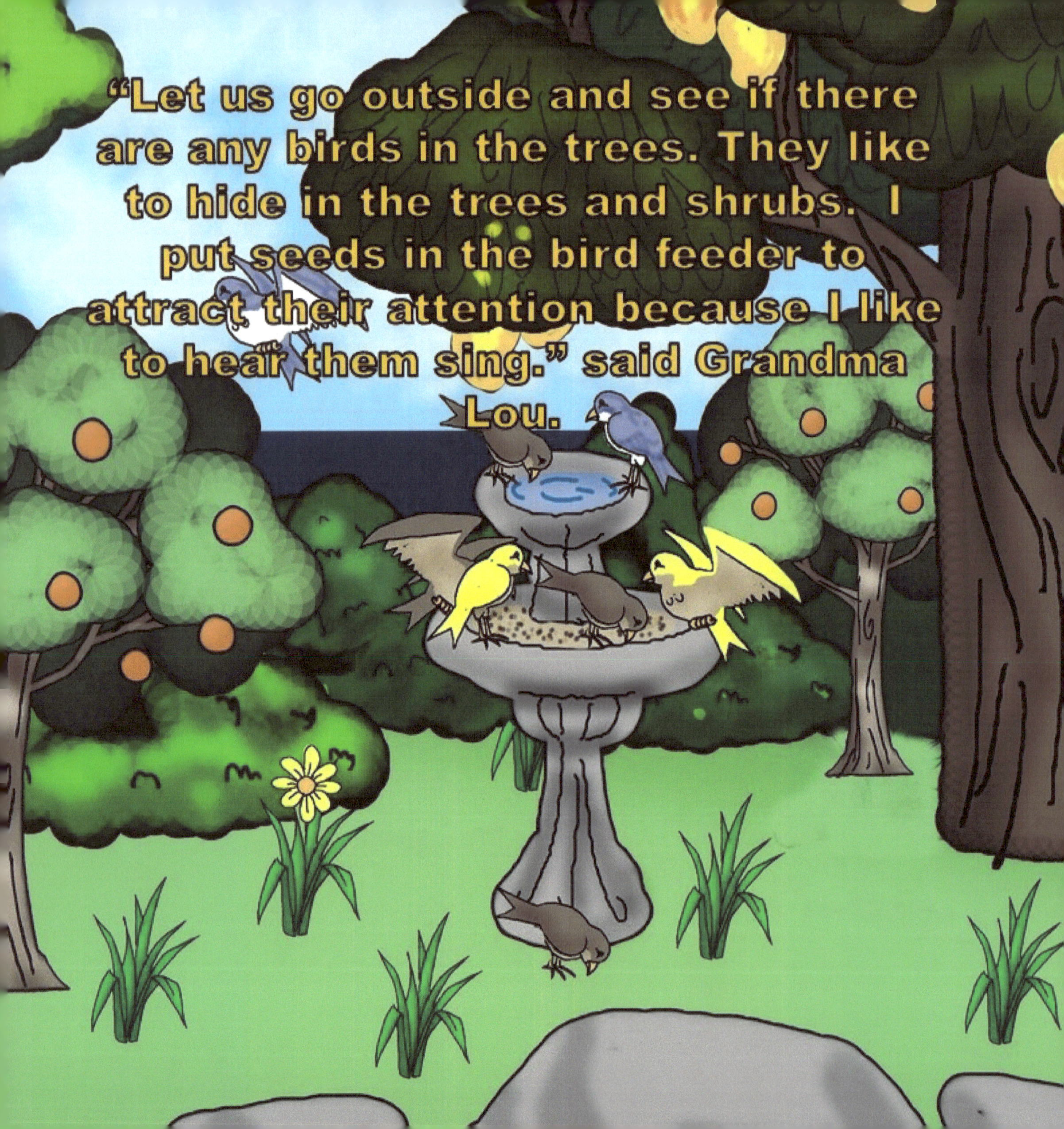
"Let us go outside and see if there are any birds in the trees. They like to hide in the trees and shrubs. I put seeds in the bird feeder to attract their attention because I like to hear them sing." said Grandma Lou.

"Do you think they will let me hold them?" asked Chatty McNally.

"They are very friendly and playful little birds, but I don't think they want to be captured. Would you like to be captured?" asked Grandma Lou.
"No Grandma, because if I were captured, I would miss seeing you, Dad, Mom, and Peter," said Chatty McNally.

"I have an idea," said Grandma Lou. "Let us get some seeds and feed them, but remember you have to be very quiet."

Grandma, Peter, and Chatty McNally
stooped down behind the shrubs,
watching the birds eat. They
watched as one little bird came near
to where they were, looked at them,
as if to say hello and then hopped
away.

Before you know it, there was a flock
of birds all pecking at the seeds.
They didn't sing again, but they were
hopping around playfully.

It was getting late, so Grandma beckoned to us that it was time to go. Grandma held on to both our hands, swinging them as we were walking.
"I love you, Grandma," said both children in unison, and "I love you more." said Grandma."

Everyone laughed and sang "Peter Come For This."
Holidays at Grandma Lou's were the best.

THE END

To receive a bracelet like the one Chatty McNally is wearing, please send a self-addressed stamped envelope, and the color of Chatty's bracelet to

Chatty Mc, Inc.
P.O. Box
678733
Orlando, FL 32867

www.chattymc.com

Now you can purchase the series of Chatty McNally Books on Amazon.com

The Child Who Tried To Vanish
Prank The Prankster
The Runaway Donkey

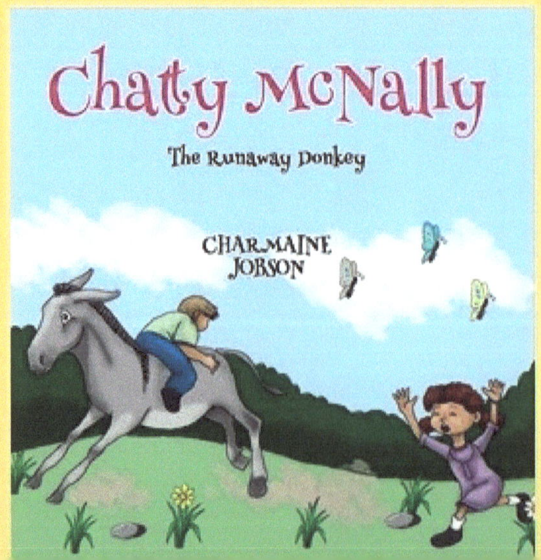